TO KILL A MOCKINGBIRD

By renine Osteen

HAIL MARY

1. Life is a hail Mary
   It goes bad, foils for many
   Strife comes, before we are ready
   And though we resist, we are not immune

2. Life is a hail Mary
   So be careful what company you keep
   Because peers have the power to influence
   The decisions we make, could lead us to doom

3. Life is a hail Mary
   We are sure about the past, but would rather sooner forget
   We experience the present, but we are numb to the lessons
   We have hope for the future, but we fear the unknown

4. Life is a hail Mary
   We live, we learn, we grow
   Heartbreaks tear our hearts like a knife
   So Jane's bad company, we will stick with Mary

5. Life is a hail Mary
   When we have we hope
   Because that simple uncharacteristic feeling
   It teaches us how to cope

6. Life is a hail Mary
   Frustrations creep on us like deadly assassins
   With one mission, steal our happiness
   We fail ourselves, we expect too much

7. Life is a hail Mary
   Ruled by uncertainties
   Nothing is really ever written in stone
   Our hearts never learn to be content

8. Life is a hail Mary
   We have plenty, it is not enough
   We have little, we learn to be grateful
   Like a deadly game of chess, we play on and on

9. Life is a hail Mary
   So don't think about death
   And all of its mysteries
   Because when it is, we are no more

10. Life is a hail Mary
    As much as people talk about destiny
    Try the impossible, to define themselves
    But are we really ever the authors of our
    story

11. Life is a hail Mary
    What a strange thing it is to be alive
    To know good and bad, and how to survive
    To have goals that drive our ambitions

12. Life is a hail Mary
    One day you will have to choose
    A partner for life, through good and bad
    So be careful of the choices you make

13. Life is a hail Mary
    That we are alive, is just a miracle
    Anything can kill us, in fact everything can
    Yet against all odds, we continue to blossom

14. Life is a hail Mary
    Sometimes simply the worst version of our
    story told
    We don't choose our homes, families,
    background
    It is like we are all pawns is someone's game

15. Life is a hail Mary
    And trust is hard to come by
    So even with so much darkness in the world
    Try to know the difference, even when the light burns for a while

16. Life is a hail Mary
    We are held to a certain standard
    We are but pieces of a bigger puzzle
    That if we go against the grain, we are whisked like chaff

17. Life is a hail Mary
    Like a bus ride that keeps us on the edge
    A hundred miles an hour, a hundred feet from a fall
    And sometimes we just wave as it passes by

18. Life is a hail Mary
    So best be your brother's keeper
    We humans are weak, we give in far too easily
    So before you judge, try to remember
    They are just people like you and me

19. Life is a hail Mary

As much as you wish, you can't really figure it out
The stars don't have our stories
We don't even have a story if not for our past

20. Life is a hail Mary
Sometimes it is enough just to be alive
People are good, but they are lost in their ways
Busy chasing dreams, but dreams stand in the way

21. Life is a hail Mary
You are my friend, I call you brother
Because it is the simple things we choose
That make our journey through life easier

22. Life is a hail Mary
Think about it, some people are rich
And some people are poor
Set to fail as much as they try
We live in a world where the many are ruled by the few
This society is broken
The system favours the glorious few

We struggle to be the few, even though it is a long shot
But if we think about it, it is the many that matter
We matter,
Our lives are full of grace
Even though they are blessed to be above us
The lord is with us, we have far fewer problems
And blessed are the fruits of hardwork
We are truly the fathers of this nation
Now, and long after our death, we will still matter

POMPOUS POMPS

1. Don't shake my hands politely
   You have perfected your greetings
   You have polluted our morals
   Always politics and never policies
   You forgot people's power got you elected
   You pretend to care but it's just a ruse
   So no, I don't need your politics or greetings
   I don't need your prayers, money or power
   Let me stay with my problems, those I can manage
   Away with you, you pompous pomps

2. You are petty people
   Probably because you have pretty little minds
   You postpone projects progress to you is a song to sing about
   Pardon us, but our ignorance has washed
   We won't play your games, pay your bills
   Forget the past or accept your presents
   This time we will do it proper, no prejudice
   Our paper hearts have been torn far too often
   Pole sana, to you politicians
   And way with you, you pompous pomps

3. Your words are a bitter pill to swallow
Your words are a bitter pill to swallow
You are too shallow to hold public office
Your problematic mouth has divided this nation time and again
Please, stop thinking you are above the law
You are not special, you don't even have the potential
This is not the high seas, we won't be ruled by pirates
Proponents of the old system, oppression is all you know
You preach peace but what your actions speak
So away with you, you pompous pomps

4. I find your bickering a pathetic call attention
It's poetic, how people like you end up where you are
Your factions represent the privileged few
While the rest of us wallow in poverty
You can't imagine the pains you cause
One day your punishment will come
I take pity on your poor souls

You have precious little time to change your ways
Away with you, you pompous pomps

5. You advocate killing of protestors
You attack the opposition like a pack of wolves
Protestant or Catholic, we all believe in the same God
Muslim or Christian, the path to righteousness is the same
Prepare, judgement for you will come sooner
You are dragging us back, we want to prosper
We won't tolerate your persistent poor performance
Promising to do better next term, you sound like a broken record
Don't forget we have a population of forty million
Finding your replacement is easy as pie
So away with you, you potbellied, rumour mongering pompous pomps.

PROPAGANDA

1. What's good for the gander, what's proper
What makes men prosper
Confidence, the power of positive thinking
There is proof in the pudding
If they can preach, if they prove to be good
If they can fix, pull themselves together
Go on drinking sprees, still pay your bills
Fix problems, lead nations to prosperity
Make fool proof plans for the future
What's good for the gander, proper
Is good for the goose, propaganda

2. What's good for the gander, what's proper
What makes men push the limits everyday
Put their countries on the maps, break records
Make the impossible possible
Paving way for the younger generations to shine
Lead their own to the promised land
Be the perfect shoulder to cry on if it all goes South
Put up with your poor attitude, show you the way

Play their part and sometimes yours too
What's good for the gander, proper
Is good for the goose, propaganda

3. What's good for the gander, what's proper
What makes men pretentious or honest
There's a possibility that this is just me thinking
But the one to beat the one has no real power
As the proverb says, barking dogs seldom bite
All people are equal, proper
Men and women are the same propaganda
What's good for the gander, proper
Is good for the goose, propaganda

4. What's good for the gander, what's proper
Men can go to parties, get wasted
And never fall victim to preying eyes
Have plenty sex, act a fool, get a number pregnant
Practice polygamy, be deadbeat fathers
Unpredictable, impossible, pretty reckless
There are consequences but they pale in comparison
What men can do women can do, proper

What men can do properly, women can do perfectly, propaganda

5. What's good for the gander, what's proper
They say perception is the name of the game
A first lady , a president, proper
A president, a puppet, potentially dangerous
A house by a man, the head, proper
A man who fades in the background, problematic
So be patient, know your man
Then play to his strengths
Don't fix pipes, or lift weights
Philosophers think feminity and masculinity
Is defined by degrees, physical attributes, not specific parts
What's good for the gander, proper
Is good for the goose, propaganda

6. What's good for the gander, what's proper
To redefine what to all genders is proper
To make sure no person is treated different
To redefine pronouns and collective nouns
If you miss putting women in crowds
Like ancient texts didn't provide numbers
All the miss will wonder at your profound ignorance

If you suggest even politely, women should cook
Then you will surely be called possessive
And such is the situation the poisons their minds
What's good for the gander, proper
Is good for the goose, propaganda

THE PROGRESS HYMN

1. Whose country is it?
   Ours
   Who pays the taxes?
   Us
   So who suffers when our economy fails?
   Us
   And who has the power to change that?
   We, the people
   And how will we do that?
   We will start a revolution
   So what do we want?
   Change
   When do we want it?
   Right now

2. Whose children get shot in the streets?
   Ours
   Who mourns and cries in grief and buries their loved ones?
   Us
   Who gets traumatized to see their dead children?
   Us
   And who has the power to stop the killing?
   We, the people

And how will we stop the killing?
We will start a revolution
So what do we want?
Change
When do we want it?
Right now

3. Let me ask, whose families sleep hungry?
Ours
Who survives on minimum wage?
Us
I asked you, who has to live like a second rated citizen?
Us
And who has the power to bring back our jobs?
We the people
How are we going to do that?
We will start a revolution
So what do we want?
Change
When do we want it?
Right now

THE INCONSPICUOUS TRUTH

1. We die by our own hands
   We have the power to change our fate
   When we are born, we are pure and innocent
   We believe, the world is ours for the taking
   Then our hearts turn black
   And we curse the life we have

2. We die by our own hands
   We struggle to be a civilized lot
   Because we are one of a kind
   We are a species like no other
   We believe the world was built for us
   Then our eyes turn green
   And we take what isn't ours

3. We die by our own hands
   We fight for the right to have equal say
   Decide our future, a future to believe in
   Because we want to live a better life
   We believe that only true leaders can bring lasting change
   Then our minds turn hollow
   And we forget all the lessons

4. We die by our own hands

As we reach for the stars, and dream of paradise
We try to perfect our life, pretend we are better off
But the more we progress, the more we derail
Because these dreams come at a cost
Then our dreams turn to poison
And choke the future we taught we would have

5. We die by our own hands
We write the future we want
Or write nothing at all, because we are scared
Scared to change because we can't be alone
We used to believe in something bigger
Then our ambitions burnt to ash
And now we are just stumbling blocks

6. We die by our own hands
Remember the spirit of independence
The dreams that built the nations
A time when all tribes united for a cause
Because we believed in the strength of unity
Then our pride turned to hatred
And we failed to be our brother's keeper

7. We die by our own hands
Change is inevitable, we know that
We think

The world moves on because of us
The truth is
The world moves on in spite of us
We believed in self preservation, of culture and religion
Then the world changed drastically
And our self preservation only served to hold us back.

EAST WEST HOME IS BEST

1. Our home is a nest
Where a bird comes to roost
Though people might look at it in jest
East west home is best

2. Our home is a fort that stands the tests
When time passes and seasons change fast
It stands towering above the rest
East west home is best

3. I miss our home, so I leave school in haste
Mother makes sure we have enough, even for guests
And that we use it well, with minimum waste
East west home is best

4. As sure as the sun rises in the East
And sets in the West
I know I will always have a place to rest
East West home is best

5. In the joys of a good home I trust
That to bad weather I need not to adjust

It comes with hard work and money that is just
East West home is best

6. If we want a party, then we are free to host
Even though we have plenty of neighbours, we invite most
And prepare a worthy and memorable feast
East West home is best

7. In the neighbourhood our house is the biggest
With many workers who work the hardest
To make sure our compound is the cleanest
East West home is best

8. People say my father is a perfectionist
After a day's work he relaxes in the Sauna's mist
I don't do so but I get the jist
East West home is best

9. My mother has a peculiar taste
She takes her time choosing and spends the least
She often calls on me to assist
East West Home is best

101

1. Think about it
Think deeply and meditate about it
Are we here for a reason?
Or is it just by default that we exist
Are we not pre-ordained to be extra-ordinary?
If we have control of our actions
If we live in this beautiful dream
And we are alive, we are progressive
We eat, we have, we love and appreciate
Is it enough?
Or are our actions just the beat in a rhythm
The rhythm of life
Are we beautiful dreamers?
Thinking we are of all things rulers
Waiting for the grim ripper
Waiting for the inevitable end
Struggling this mysterious life to mend
So that to a better place we are send
Is there such a thing
A better place where angels sing
The journey we make if we respond to the calling
So that when one life is ending
Another life is beginning

Do we have a soul?
Are we human, the children of God?
Or are we animals
And all that's special is a bigger brain

Y.O.L.O.

1. Close it out, don't let it out
Try to forget about it, scream and shout
Go out, drown out the pains
Get wasted, have high spirits
Forget about the world, go crazy
Do something stupid, get intoxicated
Drink until you black out
Dance to the rhythm of music
Wine, get down on it, feel the beat
Sense it all, take it in
Don't judge strangers, its all about the danger
Sometimes reality is stranger
So lock them up in your arms
Feel the taste of their lips, pressed on yours
Let the temperature of their body arouse you
Don't hold back, living like the night won't last
Let the euphoria sweep you
Do you feel the strength in your body
Do you feel the joy in your mind
Do you feel invincible
Forget about the world
Your troubles don't matter, not today anyway
Spend money money like you have millions
You are young, you have it all
The whole world bows down to you

You have it in the palm of your hands
Catch and release, sample the variety
Be the best version of yourself
Party until you drop dead
You are young, you are wild, you are free

MY HOME IS CALLING

1. I have been here for days
Hoping for water to quench my thirst
Company to lessen my loneliness
Praying for the waiting to stop
I need to know one thing for certain
I need to know if I will be going back
I am not made of stone
I am not an island in a sea
I have tried to keep it together this far
I have tried to hide my feelings
I have dispelled my anxious thoughts
But my mind can't think can't think of anything anymore
I close my eyes, all I see are their smiles
Faces I long so much to see again
My heartbeats for one place
A place I call home

2. I know life has to go on
I suppose it doesn't make sense to you
But I am sure I am just like you
I am also a stranger in this world
I face the same dilemmas in my life
I have many questions I ask myself
Sometimes when I am alone I think about it too

The long journey behind me
I did not choose my family
But I am lost without you
I try to be different, I try to fit in
I try to brush aside thoughts about them
I know I will see them again, some day
I know there's no genuine reason to worry
But I have failed to teach my heart that
My heart sees the world in black and white
My mind is curious and wants to explore
My heart beats for one place
A place I call home

3. I am rambling
I am conscious of the image I am creating
You probably think I am being unreasonable
If I tell you how I feel you won't understand
I wish you knew the bond I have
The memories that building holds
Have you ever been so lucky
That you feel like you cheated fate
You know, blessed beyond the sense of it
I am blessed, abundantly and beyond
I have a very big family
They teach me things, they whisper in my ears
It's all going to be alright
They stare at me like they have found gold

I know they treasure me that much
My heart misses their hugs
I miss their voices, I feel drawn to them
My heart beats for one place
A place I call home

4. It sounds strange
But I still want you to understand
The full meaning of my words
I am not like them, I am different
It's probably cruel what happened to me
After all, don't we all think it
That a hospital is such a horrible place
Especially for one like me who
As a victim of circumstances beyond my control
Had to spend every waking hour in one
But that's where you are wrong
It is not just a hospital, it is the hospital
It is not a horrible place, it is a magical place
It is where miracles happen
It is where people defy the odds
It is where my family is, it is my home
You have your home, I am sure you miss it
I do too, I miss it very much
My heart beats for one place
A place I call home

5. You dream of blue skies
I dream of white walls
You dream of furnished living room
I dream of an immaculate word
You live for the get together
I live for the morning briefings
You are entertained by the movies on T.V
I like to just sit back and watch the rush
The pitter patter of tiny feet just melt your heart
A full waiting room, happy faces makes my day
I eat at the cafeteria
I observe, I learn, more than you can imagine
Stitching is like knitting,
My many mothers teach me how to knit
I learn the medicine by heart
You do chores, I wash wards
But hey, home is home
Mine is bigger, busier, full of emotions
But I live for the thrill
Some get quiet homes, small homes
Some get the whole package
My heart beats for one place
A place I call home

6. So don't rescue me
Don't find me a home

I am at home, this is my home
I don't need a family, the one I have is enough
I am not unfortunate
I am the luckiest little person in the world
You might look and see just a working space
With doctors, nurses and patients
I look and see a big happy family
That is always open to guests
Just as you know for sure where to go
When you feel low and want to rest
When the world chews you up and spits you out
This is that place for me
This is my home, they are my family
It is my life, it is where I will always come back to
Because just like you and everyone else
My heart beats for one place
A place I call home

THE QUESTIONS WE ASK

1. The things we feel
When life comes crashing down
When all hope is lost
When it seems like the sun will never rise
And all dreams burn to ashes
And we are left at crossroads
No will to go forward
And just too tired to go back
The things we feel in our heart
When this darkness washes over us
And grief grips us like a magnet
Why do we feel the things we feel?

2. The people we love
The people we find are more than others
The people our hearts beat for
Tall, elegant, beautiful, twisted, caring
The people who are the epitome of perfection
The ones we miss every single day
The ones we can't think about enough
The ones we share with everything
The people we love
They seem to pop out of our dreams
That we have to wonder if they are not angels
Why did they come into our lives?

3. The places we call home
Cold frigid, rich, hot, extreme
They could be far away from civilization
In the heart of scorching deserts
Surrounded by nothing but an eternity of water
Right next to man eater's hunting ground
High above the ground, unsafe and abandoned
Or in swamps infested with mosquitoes
The places we call home
Lost in the deep, tragic and horrendous
Sometimes we can barely survive
Why do we love the places we call home?

4. The company we keep
Friends, buddies, bosoms, acquaintances
Some we need but don't know why
Those who charm us with their sweet words
Hold our hands when the journey takes its toll
Those whose silence we enjoy more
Those who share a special bond with us
And even though we fight, we still seek them
The company we keep
They say determines the people we become
Think about it, the difference the presence
Of just one individual can make to our lives

5. The goals we have
   Trying our best to forge our way
   Face the future head on, no take backs
   No regrets, no looking back, no backing down
   But what is the future
   How much of it is in our control
   Does our happiness depend on achieving these goals
   Are we failures if we don't, can we redeem ourselves
   The goals we have
   The gambles we take to achieve the things we want
   The pains we endure to get to the promised land
   But isn't programming ourselves equal to losing humanity

6. The choices we make
   What we wear, who we date, what we eat
   Some we grow into them
   Some just seem better alternatives
   And still some are results of general progression
   We can love, we can hate

Sometimes the line between can be stretched thin
We do different things for different reasons
The choices we make
Whether drastic or gradual erratic or necessary
Do they define us, as much as we define them?
Is it one of those infinitely circular concepts?

7. Friends talk about stuff
Lovers enjoy body contact, they like to listen
Everyone sometimes longs for company
It's our peers that influence us the most
Friends are not good role models
They care but they are not overreaching
Parents have a tendency
To automatically try to turn us into them
The days we spend, with people we know
Sometimes, time flies by so quickly
And the lines get blurred
And therein lies the problem

8. So bad friends make a bad you
Good friends make a better you
But it is not unidirectional, there's no authority
Sometimes though, it is the choices that doom us

But how do we know, that we don't know what we don't
What kind of inherent capacity solves such madness?
So that we can try to change ourselves
To be more like ourselves, less like our friends
The company we keep
The things we do, the lies we tell
The streets we walk, the dreams we chase
What if they are all just pieces of the same puzzle?

THE HIGHS AND THE LOWS

1. Life is like a tide
With the highs and the lows
Somewhere in the heart of the sea
A storm gathers, rambles and raptures
The winds push outwards
Racing for landfall
And then motions ripple
The water rises steadily in suspended rhythm
Water deserts the shores
Exposes the softer sands of the beaches
Almost as if it is bading the coastline goodbye
Ripples inwards, rises and traces back
Making landfall with a splash

2. Life is like a mountain
An expanse of land that slowly rises
Making a gradual slope
From a lower point to a higher point
And the journey up is tiresome
The winds are violent and opposite
But the journey downhill is easy
As gravity accelerates the speed of descent
Much like the hard task of getting the
managerial job
How much personal life you sacrifice

How dedicated you have to be to get a promotion
And the patience it takes to wait for your experience to count
And how easily one scandal
Can get you right back where you started

3. Life is like a season
The scorching summer of hardships
As rivers dry up across the savannah
Every single drop of water
Swallowed in the searing heat
Followed by the torrential spring of blessings
Trees wilt, become ghosts
As winter brings snow
And animals in the North Pole hibernate
Go hungry for days, survive on little
Or rivers freeze to ice across the South pole
But all is never lost
The sun will rise someday
It can't always be winter
Hold on, a breakthrough is coming

4. Life is like a day's cycle
The world spins round and round
Belly east, half the world wakes
Due West, the other half close work

But it won't be night forever
Every sky has a silver lining
And every dog has his day
It doesn't matter what you do
Or where you sleep it will dawn
As sure as the sun rises in the East
And sets in the West
A new day will begin
Some might die, it is natural, it is life
Some will wake up, better
But either way, life will go on

I HATE YOU

1. I hate you
You with your ironed suits
And expensive phones
Walking with purpose, from office to office
Leaving a trail of intoxicating perfume behind
Constantly smiling as you go along
What are you smiling at?
Who wants to see your perfect teeth?
I know you had them cleaned
Those are too white to be natural
But who the hell cares about your sophisticated clothes
Your expensive shoes or disarming smile
You must think you are better than me
Because you have a good job, that pays well
You get to go out with the pretty women
You can drive them around in your Lamborghinis
And splash all the money on them
So they can love you back
Warm your bed too
And whisper sweet nothings in your ear
you think you are so civilized
I think not
I hate how you work for eight hours a day

And think you deserve to be paid more
You are not progressive
You are not building the nation
You work in a bank owned by foreigners
That tempts people with loans they can't repay
And end up enslaving them
No, you are not a patriot
Damn you to hell and back
You who preys on the weak in society
Pollute the air with your stupid vehicles
I am sure even your stupid suits
Are the result of underpaid overworked
children
Who could be doing something better
I don't want to be like you
You arrogant useless fool
You have no morals, you are not a real person
You are nothing but a hypocrite
God will not hear your prayers
I am sure you are already destined for hell
Call me a hater if you want to
I couldn't care less what you think
You make me sick to the pits of my stomach
You give co-operations the power to play God
You do their dirty work for them
What happened to that small boy
Who always dreamt of being an actor

Who I looked up to, to become accomplished
You turned your back on us
Because you are a greedy good for nothing dimwit
And now you dare look down on me
You and your fellow scoundrels despise me
Because I had the courage to follow my dreams
You hit big time, you are a vampire
Feeding off other people's sweat
And you condemn me to poverty
You would rather spend money on American movies
I hate you with every vein in my body
You are not Kenyan, you are not even free
You don't deserve to be Kenyan
And I will not shy away from telling you
I hate you to the ends of the world
Why don't you go to the U.S.A
Join your idiotic children in your quest for vanity
How can you think you are better than me?
I am true to myself, who are you?
If not for another imbecile
That has claws dug deep in our economy
With both hands dragging us to hell
Where is your pride, you shameless traitor?

Where is your dignity?
You see, that's why I will never stop hating you
You are a disgrace to this nation
You have betrayed the blood our people bled
You have failed this nation

THE HAUNTING OF ST.PETERS

1. Here at St. Peter's seminary
The gentleman's secondary
There is a myth about things not so ordinary

2. The say in the night's stillness
Creatures from the graves' wilderness
Wander under the cover of darkness

3. I have heard such a story
Though teachers say not to worry
Sometimes when it is quiet it gets scary

4. We got to bed after our reading sessions
When I get to the dormitories I make preparations
For the next day, to avoid morning confusion

5. By six everyone is usually dead asleep
Snoring in slumber, lost in the deep
They can never tell when they start to creep

6. I have seen it before with my own eyes
The goblin from the graveside they crawl like mice
They move quietly, they don't like any surprise

7. Yesterday when I went to bed I had a lot on my mind
Sleep was elusive to find
So I sat in silence, until I saw a creature of a different kind

8. His eyes were bulging out of their sockets
And his cheeks hang in fats like pockets
He made shrill call much like a cricket

9. His skin was green and old
When he got close, I saw it had folds
Like one who had endured harshness untold

10. He was small and had sharp fingernails
And the others followed his trail
I clutched onto my blankets, afraid and frail

11. He came straight at me like he'd found a target
Jumped onto the bed, I felt his breath the closer he got
His long fingernails scratched at my blankets

12. The goblin from the graveside
His eyes and mine met in horror
As I opened my mouth to scream blue murder

13. But he jumped off and ran
Out of the doors into night
I keep thinking, he will be back again.

FREEDOM

1. This is my prayer to have and to hold
   To protect the spirit of oneness
   To have hope that a better day will dawn
   And the problems we have
   We will find a solution in the end
   This is my prayer
   To be free of the burden of hate
   To be free, to be totally free

2. This is my prayer to have and to hold
   To be free to decide our destiny
   In a future unknown
   To progress naturally through hard work and patience
   But to have the chance to work
   To be happy with our lives
   To achieve beyond our wildest dreams
   This is my prayer
   To be free of the burden of unemployment
   To be free, to be totally free

3. This is my prayer to have and to hold
   To enjoy life even though it is fleeting
   To live in peace and tranquility
   To be sure that life will be bad

To hold the keys to our own happiness
This prayer
To be free of the burden of diseases
To be free, to be totally free

4. This is my prayer to have and to hold
To have a job with security
To have insurance for when disease strike
To have everything I will ever need
To hold the keys to my own future
This is my prayer
To be free of the uncertainties
To be free, to be totally free

5. This is my prayer to have and to hold
To have a genuine partner through life
To hold my own before I depart
To have something more to live for
Another generation to carry on my name
To hold the keys of my own happiness
This is my prayer
To be free of the all the heart breaks
To be free, to be truly free

6. This is my prayer to have and to hold
To have a good home, a happy life
Some get it but let slip through their fingers

To have a long and wonderful life
To live a complete life
So that at the end, when death comes
I will know that I was alive
This is my prayer
To be free of all the dangers
To be free, to be truly free

7. This is my prayer to have and to hold
To have kindness for all
Life doesn't give us all greatness
Some roads are narrow and end suddenly
This is my prayer
To be free of the burden of pride
To have compassion
And to hold the principles of fairness in my conduct
This is my prayer
To hold the keys to how people remember me
To be great, to be truly great

PROGRESS IS

1. Progress is
Sleeping early, waking up early
A fresh mind for a productive day
A committed now for brighter tomorrow
A disciplined conscience for a happy life
A good heart that values the lessons
A big light at the end of the tunnel
A new life to carry the heritage
A steady hand to help the weak
So that at the end of the day
We all make it across the finish line
Because we live in a society
And a society is
Like a long chain with joined pieces
And we are all pieces of a big puzzle
Our life is incomplete unless we belong
The people that raise us have a bond with us
We must realize that
A chain is only as strong as its weakest link

2. Progress is
Three steps forward, one step backward
Gradual change that makes the biggest of
differences
Growth that can be sustained

Good systems that empower achievement
Equity for all, regardless of status
Faith in the youth, they are the future
Adequate preparation for a future unknown
Good ethics for a stable growth

3. Progress is
Seeing past the outside, understanding the full truth
We all matter
We are descendants of a common tree
We walk on two
We have two eyes at the front of our face
We walk upright to see ahead
We have hair on our body, not fur or scales
We speak a language with sounds and letters
We are transient
We know our surroundings
We believe in something
If we were to intermarry
We would birth healthy offsprings
Our internal anatomical structure is the same
The only difference is the colour of our skin
The foundations of our religion
The creed of our ancestors
And the nationality of our fathers
Progress is seeing past these little differences

4. Progress is
Working hard wherever we are
Upholding good principles regardless of our conditions
Rising up for the well being of our kind
Finding in our heart, to forgive our offenders
Being charitable, we all have more than we need
Embracing leadership as a chance to serve
Protecting our environment for future generations
Having what we need, not what we can
Speaking out against ills in the society
Because silence is consent
Doing nothing but the best
We have great power, to look over the world
There were others before us, who ruled just like us
They understood their place in the hierarchy of life
There will be others like us, to inherit this world
And our responsibility is to leave this world
Better than we found it
Yes, we rule this world but we must know this philosophy
With great powers comes great responsibilities

5. Progress is
Changing with the times
Knowing that change is inevitable
Because ultimately, change changes everything
The landscape has changed
Technology is the engine that drives economy
Man has achieved the impossible
He can in the sky
He can defy gravity and move at great speeds
That is change
And those who won't change
Almost always gets left behind
It is not survival for the fittest
But yes, there is such a thing as an urban jungle
The world is connected
We can pretend to be different
Try to force the world to change to our wants
But it will never happen
We can say that in the interest of self
preservation
We will limit our society to our literature
We will shape our society with our words
But ultimately it is a losing war
In a global market, international stories
Those which connect to many
Cut across thousands of cultures
Will always perform best

6. Progress is
   Understanding our responsibility
   In shaping the nation
   It is true that for real change to happen
   It takes a revolution
   A revolution takes a movement
   Driven by a deep hunger for change
   Not afraid to upset the status quo
   It can't always be business as usual
   We can't bicker and fight over unimportant issues
   While our country burns
   So where do we start
   People say it starts with elections
   I think not
   I think it starts with challenging the status quo
   Engineering a great withdrawal
   From backward systems
   Setting ourselves apart from their recurrent failures
   And doing what we deem progressive
   Leadership is not given, inherited
   That is just politics
   Leadership is taken
   So it is time to take back our country

MY HEART

1. My heart
   My simple fragile heart
   Will not survive another heartbreak
   Yet I still believe in love
   We risked everything for happiness
   Even though I knew nothing lasts forever
   It was enough to feel even for a moment
   To live like we were in a fairytale

2. My heart
   My irrational reckless heart
   Does not know never to take a gamble
   Because love is the biggest gamble
   My reckless heart doesn't shy away
   It searches and searches, hoping to find
   The meaning of life in the power of love
   The power that makes us then breaks us

3. My heart
   My defiant stubborn heart
   Wants you in spite of your flaws
   Which are many and glaring
   Which will certainly be our doom
   Trust a desperate man to ignore all the signs
   The universe gives to stay away

It is hope that really kills us
Because the person they are
And the perfect little creations in our mind
Are never really the same

4. My heart
My broken soulful heart
Holds on to a past that has long passed
Dreams of a future like the past
Doesn't know the past is gone it rests in the dust
And the future will never be the same
And you will never be mine
Your path and mine are destined not to meet

5. My heart
My vicious avenging heart
Will not rest until you are mine again
My resenting heart, full of pain
Controlling and manipulating
Wants you to suffer as much as I did
Even though it longs for you
The scars are too deep to overcome

6. My heart
My wonderful naïve heart
That is too big for the world

Now look what happened
The world has betrayed it again
The heart that gives and never receives
And never learns from the cruel lessons
See how it crumbles in dismay again
Betrayed by the one we loved so much

7. My heart
My one and only heart
Now here we are again
Abandoned and suicidal
Lost and confused
I could have sworn I knew this day would come
In fact I am surprised it took this long
Would it have ended any different?
People are mean and selfish
Now it is just you and me
In the silence that defines our existence
How I pray that one day
I will be enough for you

FRACTURED

1. You are my dream, my nightmare
   You are the voice that wakes me up at night
   Keeps me staring into empty space
   The darkness I keep close to my heart
   My addiction
   The poison that destroys my soul
   Loving you is a sin, I know
   But if I burn, we burn together

2. You are the uneasiness that chokes my heart
   The anger that rattles my patience
   Fear that stirs the hairs on my body
   Pleasure that drives me to tears
   My everything
   The sun of my mornings, the moon of my nights
   Loving you is a sin, I know
   But if I burn, we burn together

3. You are the whisper that pulls me closer to hell
   The heartbreak that tears me to pieces
   Shiny fragments of my heart scattered like glasses
   Fractured, never to be whole again
   My obsession

The constant thought that colonizes my
existence
Loving you is wrong, I know
But if I burn, we burn together

4. You are a temptation I can't resist
A picture forever etched in my brain
A flawed perfection, beauty in a beast
The biggest mystery I will never solve
My better half
The other half that hides in the shadows
Loving you is a sin, I know
But if I burn, we burn together

5. You are the misery I have to live with
The devil that crushes my soul
The angel that smiles at me
Stab me in my heart then kiss me
You are my fire
That keeps me warm but burns if I get cosy
Loving you is a sin, I know
But if I burn, we burn together

6. You are the desire I cannot control
The queen who rules my heart with an iron fist
Your side never known with wars you wage
You are for, you are against

You are a force-field
That with fury, curves my heart inside out
Loving you is a sin, I know
But if I burn, we burn together

THEY CRIED WOLF

1. They cried wolf
   It was the end of civilization as we knew it
   The stage was set
   The fall out was imminent
   After years of what most suspected
   Was a fragile outward world peace
   The arms race began

2. They cried wolf
   As more nations got their fingers on the trigger
   Weapons of mass destruction
   The savvy remote controlled fighter jets
   Laser guided missiles
   And even the robotics program
   That had taken a blind leap into the future

3. They cried wolf
   When the North Korea nation
   Started experimenting with nuclear energy
   They said the apocalypse was coming
   And we waited
   Hoping we would somehow be ready

4. They cried wolf
   When a big mass of space dust

A fractured remnant of a meteor
Burning brightly like a wishing star
Fell out of the depths of the unknown
They said it would eclipse the sun
And wipe out all civilization

5. They cried wolf
As the former superpowers
Met at crossroads again
With deep seated mistrust
And irreconcilable political differences
Started shouting murder across the borders
History was repeating itself
A sovereign nation had just lost its territory
The cold war was here to haunt the world
And the Syrian crisis was getting worse by the day
The news cycles had all the ingredients
Of a world on the brink of war

6. They cried wolf
The son of a patriot
Who had a score to settle
His eyes on the prize
But vengeance on his mind
They said he had hands of steel
And he would rule with an iron fist

And his journey to the throne
Was going to be the beginning of the end

7. They cried wolf
The stories gave us shivers
We all shuddered at the thought
A wanted man on the helm
The fallout it would bring
The big court of law
Would rain down sanctions like snow
This struggling nation would be no more

8. They cried wolf
The country would soon collapse
It is inevitable they say
As everyone turns to his own
The spirit of nationalism is long dead
The road to recovery is shrouded in the unknown
We are not one
We are just pieces, incompatible and unstable
We are a ticking time bomb
One election away from a complete meltdown

9. So we look to the future with dread
Any day could be the last
Any defiant act could be the one

The last straw that breaks the camel's back
We are skeptical but we can feel it
The tension in the air, the familiar script
We know we have been here before
We can see the winds charging
It has taken centre stage in the news
It could happen
It well within the realm of possibilities
In fact, mathematically, it should happen
A storm is coming
We don't know when
But we can certainly feel the gusts of wind

THE COMPANY WE KEEP

1. Magic words, winding paths
Daredevil, beautiful dreamers
Strangers in paradise, lost souls
Heartbreakers, soul seekers
The company we keep
Determines the people we become

2. Jilted lovers, angry citizens
Know it alls, sarcastic punks
Radioheads, born frees, care frees
Conditioned, criminal masterminds
The company we keep
Determines the people we become

3. Illustrious, dominating, abusive
High spirited, stubborn, open minded
Non-challant, charming, disarming
Social, inthrovert, high class
The company we keep
Determines the people we become

4. Paranoid, short wired, overbearing
Self centred, self righteous
Arrogant, ignorant, entrepreneurial
Thinkers, doers, sayers

The company we keep
Determines the people we become

5. Conflicted, poignant, confident
Self aware, sycophant, rebel
Napoleon's complex, law abiding
Philosophical, unapologetic
The company we keep
Determines the people we become

6. Alcoholic, drug abusers
Risk addiction, gamblers
Life of the party, trainwreck
Brave, hollow, cowardly
The company we keep
Determines the people we become

7. Bossy, sexy, sassy, classy
Casual, official, unusual
Champion, cheat, unsportsman
Cold, calm, collected, crude
The company we keep
Determines the people we become

8. Clumsy, social climbers, principled
Christian, lively, comical
Competent, dependable, flip flopper

Considerable, adorable, responsible
The company we keep
Determines the people we become

9. Consistent, constructive, destructive
Positive, negative, progressive
Kind hearted, hopeless romantic
Elegant, relevant, energetic
The company we keep
Determines the people we become

10. Corrupt, critic, enthusiastic
Back biter, honest, loyal
Pretender,, fanatic, delinquent
Gentle, generous, hooligans
The company we keep
Determines the people we become

THOUGHTLESS

1. Another pose for that moment of clarity
   The quest to find answers brings more questions
   Fate has a fatal lesson for us
   In a world of dreams and demons, faith and fate
   And moments when we chose to trust
   But humanity is weak, thoughtless as we go along

2. Another pose for that moment of clarity
   Defining the bounds of this unreal world
   Is this the course for getting beyond the other realms?
   Another dreamer standing in the midst of skeletons
   Shouting fortune for the dead world to pay heed
   Why bother when our thoughtless minds repulse

3. Another pose for that moment of clarity
   To the utter surprise that life is ending
   Ghosts wandering through the streets of civilization

An embrace to the dead world when the beat stops
The difference between reality and illusion
And we find ourselves in this fatal spur of moment

4. Another pose for that moment of clarity
A paper trail to another reality within our past
The magic soon begins to fade
And the oddity of the moment lingers forever
A heart of stone to smite the wisdom
There's death in every inch of our dilatory choices

5. Another pose for that moment of clarity
An approbation of the best step forward
The world is dying in the heat of past errors
The life that is left seeping to infinity as before
Thoughtless as we are the mission to a suicide pact
Derelicts of the fast pace of the life train

6. Another pose for that moment of clarity
In the end none of that mattered to us
There was always life, the candle burning bright
Our shadows skating the horizons of change
Something so different with humanity

Death looming in the heart of the night

7. Another pose for that moment of clarity
   As our thoughtless reality is going sour
   The brevity of the last legions is now a lost cause
   There is the moment of desperation to face
   The ground breaking from end to end
   And caskets piling the streets we called home before

8. Another pose for that moment of clarity
   Seeking the answers to the proverbial questions
   There is shortage of blood as thirst increases
   The sun an obstacle to the perfection of life
   Living in dreams and dying in reality
   As we die hard, thoughtless and thoughtless again

ALL MY LITTLE CHILDREN

1. Shine a light
   To those who are oppressed
   Those whose lives others have messed
   Even if they aren't impressed
   It is just enough they are not stressed
   Help them forget those who have passed
   So that their pains can be eased
   Shine a light
   All my little children
   Let the whole world see it
   Shine a light
   Like a bright star in the night sky

2. Shine a light
   When good is done to you, pay it forward
   Never expecting any reward
   Don't be wayward, act kind, don't be a tard
   And even if no one appreciates don't be sad
   Always be glad
   Those who think only of themselves are selfish and mad
   For no man is an island, and a hand that sows bad
   In the end will reap bad
   So shine a light

All my little children
Shine it for all the world to see
Shine a light
Like a bright star in the night sky

3. Shine a light
Like the Nothern star
Guide the lost down the path of redemption
So that even if they lose their lives
They will gain their soul
Teach with your heart
Don't be afraid to reach new heights
Hold their hands, they may be weak now
But it is your strength that keeps them going
So shine a light
All my little children
Shine it for the whole world to see
Shine a light
Like a bright star in the night sky

4. Shine a light
The world needs to see the truth
The lies they tell themselves hurts them
The warnings they ignore will come back to haunt them
What they call progress is losing way
Ultimately all their little sins will build

So that their perfect little world will come crushing down
Can you hear the countdown has already began
They could lose it all
So shine a light
All my little children
Teach the world how to preserve the future
Carry the message with the strength of your words
Shine a light
Like a bright star in the night sky

5. Shine a light
Addiction is like a black hole
That swallows even the brightest future
It is a slow disease
That affects most of us
With little or no symptoms
Eating lives from the inside out
Leaving skeletons of people
Who don't realize they are dying
Lift them up from their troubles
The world assumes their pains
Casts a shadow of doubt on their cries
But there's still hope for them
They need to believe in something
So that in the end they will find their way

So shine a light
All my little children
So that the whole can see
Shine a light
All my little angels
Like a bright star in the night sky

DEEP SCARS

1. The deep scars define our existence
Like shadows that walk with us
Heavy burdens that weigh us down
The pain capture our existence
The unforgettable past we try to run from
Will always come back to haunt us

2. The deep scars define our existence
No they don't hold the lessons
That's not how it works
They are just things that happened
That we often pretend didn't
So that we will trudge on
Towards a brighter future
One with cohesion and prosperity

3. The deep scars define our existence
We might not say it but we always remember
How our leaders destroyed what we built
Leaders, that is political correctness
Jomo and his clowns destroyed our nation
Reduced our proudest moment
The milestone that marked freedom
To our biggest regret
4. The deep scars define our existence

They are like a chemical mixture
That burns rapidly, expands and becomes unstable
But remains contained in closed space
And on the outside it might look okay
But on the inside our heart breaks at every turn
So let me be the first to speak the truth
The whole truth and nothing but the truth

5. The deep scars define our existence
The past years have brought no solace
Every five years we exercise our rights
But we will never achieve progress
Until we are truly free
Yes, we chased the masters and celebrated
But we are still slaves to the system

6. The deep scars define our existence
Colonialism is alive and kicking in Kenya
And this is how I will break it down
What is colonialism?
When a particular group advocates supremacy
So that even if they preach equality
They always get the best and leave less for the rest
So white people or no white people
Kenya is still in the grip of colonialism

Two tribes have colonized the rest
More than fifty years after independence
They control the instruments of power
They own the greater per centage of wealth
They elect who they want
And the system always favours them

7. The deep scars define our existence
It is not a blanket judgement
In fact not all from the chosen tribe benefit
That would have been far too obvious
Impractical even
But the minority few elite benefit
The landlords, and big money investors
They get more than they deserve
So at the end of the day really
Down here at the grassroots
We are all fighting a common enemy

8. The deep scars define our existence
You think we don't know
We are wiser than you give us credit
We know the society is broken
The divide and conquer philosophies you use
They have destabilized the nation
And even though there is peace, all is not well
Two tribes cannot rule a nation of forty two

We can't go another term without real change
We want a nation
An inclusive, progressive, non tribal nation
And if you ask me
It begins with the two tribes
The Kalenjin and the Kikuyu
Taking a step back from power
So in reality, they hold the power
To make us or break us

MOMENTUM

1. In the physical world it is rare to have a backward momentum
   Because that defies the natural state of being
   An object at rest is not functional
   But if you apply a force then it moves
   Energy from you is deferred to the object
   So an object at rest will always remain at rest
   Unless something changes its initial state

2. To have a backward momentum
   An object initially at rest moves
   Achieving forward progression then backtracks
   For example a vehicle pushed down a valley
   Achieves forward momentum
   Because its wheels catapult it
   In the general direction of gravity flow
   If the same vehicle were to reach a hill
   Because of the momentum gained
   It would climb the hill
   But only to the point where
   The momentum gained becomes less than the gravity drive
   In which case the gravity drive will force it back
   Thus achieving a backward momentum

3. So to have a backward momentum
There has to be an object that is manipulated
By two opposite forces on the same plane
That is the physics aspect of it
I will not bore you with colloquial nonsense
Instead I will try to put it all into perspective
So that it will make sense

4. So what would a vehicle need
To overcome its limits
Our vehicle needs technological advantage
Something that gives it greater mathematical
odds
Our vehicle needs an engine
Making the initial force greater than the gravity
drive

5. The backward momentum
The systems that force progress backwards
The outdated systems that stagnate the
economy
In the quest for total freedom
We have forgotten we live in a global village
Trading surpasses geographical borders
And language barriers
So can we say something written is too western
Has no place in the African market

Can we say only what we write
What we consider to be African
Is the only material that has influence over society
Wouldn't it be a big lie
If we don't publish Western influenced books
That would do well in a global market
Aren't we like gravity, forcing a backward momentum
That eventually ends in stagnant careers
If we don't change with the times
Can we blame anyone for a poor literature industry
Can we blame anyone if we end up with
An equally poor film industry
What will it take for you to see
That we are the architects of our own failure

THE DEFIANT RACE

1. Capture this
Fossil fuels cause global warming
Meaning a century ago, global warming
Would have been a problem to be imagined
So what changed
In the quest for global supremacy
Somewhere between the two world wars
Man took a leap into the future
It was a bright future
Looking through the looking glass
What he saw was real change
A global world
That defied time and space
A carriage that travelled faster than the horse
The engine that welcomed the future
The motor vehicle
Class and comfort, reliability and convenience
Breathing toxic fumes that poison the air we breathe
Somehow sustaining this dream
The thing that defined the future
Became more important than breathing
Or protecting the future itself
But we are the defiant race
The more we build, the more we destroy

So on and on we build

2. Capture this
We used to live apart
We were part of nature
We lived in the wilderness
We were in every aspect the same as other animals
But we were not really the same
As we soon realized we were special
We could make weapons to use for the hunt
It was a more efficient way to live
Then we discovered fire
Probably the second milestone that set us apart
We had clothes for cold weather
And we had fire to cook and keep us warm
We were truly remarkable creatures
Then we discovered language
Because language equaled unity
And unity was strength
We started living in communities
It was easier to hunt and protect ourselves
But with society came differences
With differences came disagreements
With disagreements came quarrels
And when there was no solution we fought
So the same weapons we used to hunt

We used to shed our own blood
And kill our own kind
What a progressive lot we were
Traditional weapons like knives were good
But they killed far fewer people
So we invented the arrows
They were still not effective enough
People still survived
We upgraded to poison tip arrows
We moved away from the wild
We started living in societies
We learnt the need to train
And arm a specific section of our society
To always be ready for war
We created warriors,
But there was still need for more bloodshed
So we created guns, bullets, travelling at the speed of sound
Impossible to miss deadly on impact
We still longed for bloodshed
We created machine guns, grenades and landmines
Then came world war II
We knew we had to do more
Find a way to kill more people in less time
We tried our hands at biological warfare
Anthrax wiped out a lot of people

We knew we were creating our own death
Weapons that killed people like us
Could and would kill us too
So we went bigger and badder
Because we are the defiant race
We remain numb to the lessons
As a species, we are our own worst nightmare
We created the apocalypse
We created the atomic bomb
We are the defiant race
The more we build the more we destroy
So on and on we build

3. Capture this
So we know different places
Are suited for different species of animals
We are the mighty humans
The ones that rule the earth,
We can live anywhere
We build our homes and grow our food
We domesticate our prey and build walls
To keep out what we don't want
But other animals
Do well in their own natural habitats
We do well in cities with skyscrapers
Plenty of water and amenities
Away from natural disasters

And since we have far fewer enemies
And we have the means to fight the few we do
We have blossomed
We have grown exponentially
And we have all tried to find our place
Carve out a portion of this earth under our
name
Because we are greedy some more than others
Have land we couldn't possibly need
Creating a manmade land shortage
And since we are the defiant race
We have cleared out most of what was left
To protect the other species that live with us
Leading to mass extinction of entire families
Sometimes even entire species
Which leads to an unbalanced eco-system
But we are the defiant race
The more we build the more we destroy
So on and on we build

THE NARRATIVE

1. So this is the narrative
I am supposed to say because I am of sound mind
I am a proponent of the peace initiative
I love and respect all people equally
In spite of religion, political affiliations race or sexual orientation
The world is fine
How I know, at least nobody dies
Not because of the greed of others
It is okay to be gay
Even though the Bible forbids it
Our God is a loving God
And he loves all of his children the same
He made us all, he knows our desires
Democrats and republicans are the same
There is no racism in the world
Europe is progressive because of hard work
In a strong, fair global market
That doesn't favour any nations
All races are equal, and the whole world supports that
People should exercise their rights
Even if Trump gets elected as president
There is no racism even if America's next

Forty presidents are all white
There's no tribalism in Kenya even if
The Kalenjin and the Kikuyu
Rule for another a half a century
Russia is helping with the war in Syria
Both opposition and Isis are destabilizing the nation
But Assad is key to peace
Europe has a right to close its borders to refugees
Ruto was not involved in post election violence
It was all Raila's plot to get back at him
Even though he has no say in international court
And in fact advocated for local tribunals
All Kenya's presidents were progressive
Even though they have managed to cultivate
Tribalism and inequality
North Eastern has no right to secede
Even though everyone knows it has been abandoned
Ever since independence
The U.S.A had genuine reasons to invade sovereign states
Even though it destabilizes world peace
So all in all there's nothing wrong with the world

BUILDING THE NATION (FOR MY OWN)

1. I built a little nation in a great land
   I build a nation for all my children
   In the middle of a forest of lush green
   An oasis away from scorched sand
   They had plenty if not all
   They would blossom in the new nation
   It would be paradise for them
   They wouldn't need to know what hunger is
   I am a builder
   And I built this nation for my own

2. I built a little nation in a great land
   I built it with my own two hands
   If you touch them the soreness is evident
   I carried the stones that were the foundation
   All across the scorching desert
   It was a place where we would start over
   It was the promised land
   I am a builder
   And I built this nation for my own

3. I built a little nation in a great land
   I built it with my own money
   I had to close my empire to get enough

I had to pay the ungrateful workers
House their hordes of children and feed them
I did it all for you
Because I knew you descended from greatness
I knew you would one day be prosperous here
I am a builder
And I built this nation for my own

4. I built a little nation in a great land
I built it with my own books
I did my part in building the nation
They brought the future to me
Tiny little minds that I molded into great thinkers
I built the foundation, I prepared the future
So that one day, when they look back
They will know education is the key
I am a builder
And I built this nation for my own

5. I built a little nation in a great land
I built it with the rules I passed
There's no civilization if there are no rules
I led my people to the promised land
A place where they could dream and be free
I penned the road map to a good future

I gave them hope, a new home, something to believe
They held onto my words, they were inspired
I am a builder
And I built this nation for my own

6. I built a little nation in a great land
I built it with my steady hands, seeds and a plough
I charted the weather and planned for years
I picked the perfect spot
Where the land was fertile and would yield tenfold
It is the basics, a hungry nation is a dead nation
I brought them this far
They are healthy and happy because of my efforts
I single handedly nurtured the nation
Like a little kid watching over it
My attention unwavering
I planted seeds of greatness
I knew it would take time but some day
One day it would blossom
I am a builder
And I built this nation for my own

7. I built a little nation in a great land

There is no use for a man to gain the whole world
Only to lose his soul
Yes, the important intangible consciousness
That shapes our thoughts and actions
I don't mean to preach
But I think it is fair to say
That I built a great nation in a little land
I led my people into the light
Peace, good sense, social responsibility
I have watched my people blossom
And they are happy living in God's grace
I am a builder
And I built this nation for my own

THE THRONE

1. One day I woke up
I found I was in a dream
My eyes were opened but my sight was compromised
I was in a very big house
I had very elegant furniture
It was almost like I had won the lottery
On the stand beside the window
A humanitarian golden statue
Real gold, soft in my hands, a marvelous sight
I was struck with a sense of accomplishment
The floor was tiled and carpeted
The interior design was exquisite
It had to have been done by a professional
That must have cost a fortune
Then again practically everything around
Must have been real only by the imaginations
Of my blurred dream world reality
I put on my robes
Kissed my smoking hot wife good morning
She smiled at me
The gentle corners tilting her perfect lips upwards
She didn't stir
I stepped into the shower

For a cosy sensational gripping warm morning bath
It was a strange thing
Water, defying gravity, at man's command
So I was fresh and ready for another big day
Interviews and more interviews
My movie was hitting the big screens
Of course that was the highlight of everyone's day

2. I am a king on a throne
Not the traditional boring type
I don't get subjects with whips and taxes
I get money from them
Because I am irresistible
Yes, I must be living in a dream
To be put on a pedestal
Higher than any mortal man should be
Worshipped like a god
I am more of god, it makes sense
I am the reason theaters get sold out
I am the life of the industry
Bigger than life, eloquent, elegant
I am everyone's dreams personified
I am the mouth piece of the top one percent
I advocate, I sell, I am a phenomenon
A force of nature

I scan my house and wonder
How did I get here
How extremely special could I have been
It has nothing to do with luck
I go through my day's program
As a limousine pulls up outside
It has enough room for ten
But it only carries one
I have one endorsement after another
Big co-operations, they pay me to connect
I am the wild card in the sales game
I can make believe anything
Because my fans adore me

3. I am here on the throne
I am on top of the world
I am the top one percent of the one percent
I am the mouthpiece of the money makers
I am like a chameleon
I have mastered well the art of blending in
Real life, a dream there's no difference
My life is a movie in continuity
My every life choice is analyzed
They anticipate every life decision I make
They send me global birthday wishes
Everyone knows when I was born
When I go somewhere, that place

Whatever it is, becomes famous
I am the head of the monster
The Hollywood monster
I am the face that distracts you
From your real life problems
I can make you dream, laugh
Work you like a puppet
I am the one who will talk you into eternal debt
The poster child for pollution, violence
It's just a movie
Just look deep into my eyes
Let reality fall away, you are feeling drowsy
At the count of three
I will snap my fingers and you will feel light
A heavy burden lessened from your shoulders
The burden of reality
Welcome to my world, look around
Tell me what you see

WHEN THE NINE LIVES ARE OVER

1. Cats have nine lives
It is impossible to see how
But the myth goes way back
I think people think cats have nine lives
Because they live an impossible life
They live on the fringe of reality
They defy gravity, they always land on their feet
That's the hardest thing
That when life deals you a blow
Or in a more likely scenario you self destruct
Can you always land on your feet

2. The first lease of life
Remember when you were little
You were blissfully ignorant
Surrounded by a world of strange things
Things that could be explored
Things that had to be explored
You gave your mother a headache
She couldn't let you stray far from sight
You were always up to no good
Putting everything in your mouth
It didn't matter if they were dirty or stinking
And then one day you strayed too close to the edge
You were somehow aware of the danger

But because you were clumsy you fell
Two stories down, with nothing but cold hard ground
To receive you, probably to end it all
The pain is one of those memories
That just won't fade away
When you opened your mouth to scream
All you could manage was a silent resonance
Before the heart breaking, ear shattering, death defying scream
And your mother's shuffling feet
Running towards you, panic stricken
Five months in the critical wards
Every bone in your body shattered
Yet you survived
It is a miracle the doctors said, it to be a miracle
They released you, back to your life
And after another year of readjustment
That tragic chapter seemed like just a blip
Not enough to stop the momentum of life

3. The second lease of life
You were coming of age
Trying to differentiate between complex emotions
Your mind boggled
The world was moving too fast
There were so many voices in your head
Life had long since assumed
An unwavering rhythm

The blood rush, the flood gates of emotions
You saw the world through different lenses
You tried to cope with it all
When you were lost in background time and again
The world was a cruel place
And as much as you tried to fit in
Your place was never really defined
Until him, until he came along
With his dashing hazel eyes and a confident poise
Muscular body and athletic gait
He was barely walking on earth like everyone else
He was impossibly perfect
Do you remember that smile
That you just folded away and placed in a fort
Something to get you going
And the joy you had learning
That you were not totally invisible to him
So he was handsome
And had the wits about him too
And when he reassuringly held your head in place
Because you had overdone the alcohol
And you felt a spark, an ignition
That set your heart to start beating again
This was more than love at first sight
And then that kiss
You still had poison on your lips

And the damning stench hot on your breath
And he still kissed you
And all you could think from then on
Was just how it was the best three seconds
The seconds that really defined your existence
Then it was just you and him
As the world watched you
Through the smiles and the firsts
First kiss, first day over, first cuddling
All building to that ecstatic climax
Remember you were so happy you thought you would die
Just you and him
A moment that defined your maturity
It didn't last
Everything slowly started falling apart
He became distant
That magical connection started fading away
You still needed him
But he didn't need you
At first it was just a vague feeling
At the back of your mind
Then it was no longer just your paranoia
It became too real too first
You didn't know what to do
So you confronted her, the other girl in the picture
From then on it was a downhill drag
You could feel the end coming
Still you kept hope, had to keep hope

It was the only thing
That was holding together your fragile heart
Then he shattered it
When you heard the words it was all too real
And in spite of the premonitions you had
It was like a grenade that exploded in you
It left a deep scar, it just couldn't heal
It was all black, dark and scary
And cold and lonely, it was hell
There was nothing there
Your broken heart didn't hold any meaning
Just like your empty life that became a shell
You stopped thinking, stopped eating, stopped living
Death suddenly seemed like a better option
The voices in your head
The unruly crowd rallied you
Admittedly five hundred could have a lot
But in your new twisted reality
It was good for the strong medicine
That you downed in one gulp
That tied knots in your stomach
Made you feel again, anger and anguish
As you rolled on the floor writhing
Foaming in your mouth, screaming in agony
And it all ended in black
It surely had to be the end
Black dreams, twisted fantasies
The hazel eyed wonder that wrote that chapter
White walls, two by two hands of blue

Sheep being led to a slaughterhouse
The busy place, sharp things, undesirable objects
That numb feeling, a burning sensation
Those eyes that had more pain than yours
And the tiny hands that gripped you
Like they were afraid to let go
Light as air, drowning in your own head
The moment when reality was fractured
The forward momentum, wheels on the pebbled floors
The agonizing pain
You still survived

4. The third lease of life
You told yourself never again
You made a promise
But it happened again, like a scripted replay
So afterwards you grew cold
That part of you that used to believe
That part just feasled out
You, the child of the world
The problems on your back
You were your own worst enemy
You looked to the future
Gave the world no thought at all
The world was damned
For a brief moment you ceased to exist
The step father drama
You took a step away from it

Pen to paper, you tried to shape the blurred images
You tried to imagine a perfect world
You still had it, the friends and all
You had learnt an important lesson
Life wa fleeting, people will disappoint
So you forged a shield to guard your heart
You were the life of the party
It was a fresh beginning
A new perspective on life
The alcohol made you numb
And empty stares defined your life
You saw yourself through the eyes of the world
A far cry from the girl you used to be
You closed the pages of the books
Got an E, crushed your mother's spirit
You taught yourself not to feel
It was the thrill that drove you
Being numb to everything that was real
The fast electronic music became your heartbeat
You stopped feeling, started living
You were a complexity of personalities
Not afraid to express yourself
Not willing to remain obsolete in the background
Not afraid to experiment with your life
But it wasn't the speed of life that ended it all
It was the sleek Lamborghini going at a hundred
Swaying across all three lanes

Under your drunken stewardship
You were the captain of your soul
Your soul was a lost ship
Like tales of old
You went down with the ship
The sequence of events from mild awareness
To panic, to being totally airborne, wheels up
Turning through the air, the fatal collision
The broken bridge, the bangs, the free fall
And the splash as you hit the water head first
Still tied to your seats
Another disappointing ending
Another close brush with death
Another year at the critical ward
You saw it in her eyes
Though she still cared, she was giving up
Doctors said it was a miracle you made it

5. The fourth lease of life
Then came the headache of trying to explain
Three different deaths by your own hand
The lawyer said it could be a capital offence
The principle had had about enough
And sent you packing, exiled forever
For a while you were famous
You were the cautionary tale
But life had to go on
New school, new friends, old you, old habits
The recurrent warnings
The fall out with teachers

You were like a walking hydrogen bomb
School could barely contain you
Like everyone else you wanted more
School was just holding you back
You could have it all
It was time for a different game
Time to play the damsel in distress
Let your prince charming save you
Rich old, desperate and lonely
It could be done, you could be the one
You would upstage his sick wife
Make him feel young, vibrant, needed again
It was a perfect plan
It was seamlessly executed
The only thing between you and the Promised Land
Was the old queen herself
She watched and waited
She assessed but didn't really engage
Then she gave you a warning
It took more than harsh words to rattle your spirits
So the stage was set
The brewing pot of discontent boiled over
It was fatal and unexpected
The poison in the food
Days after your name was included in the will
You just got what you wanted
A seventy per cent share of a billion worth empire

Then you watched it all go up in flames
When the sirens shattered the silence
And you were walked away in cuffs
Now you even got a nickname
For being a notorious news items
Life imprisonment, the charges stuck
The old hag had successfully managed
To screw you over
The blackwidow, that's what you were called
The girl who was too big for life
With one pending manslaughter case
And a confirmed homicide case against you
And you were condemned
To spend the rest of your life behind bars
Life as you knew it was over
You were a celebrity for all intents and purposes
The famous blackwidow, a name spoken across the country
Just what was so special about you
A tiny quivering bag of bones, you didn't belong
They made sure you knew their point
When they mauled you mercilessly,
It could just as well have been a wild bear attack
Even the sick bay said it was too much for you
And once again in your short life span
You found yourself surrounded by the familiar faces in mask
Your life hanging by a thread
Hoping to rest, to finally rest in peace

6. The fifth lease of life
   Started that day your mate
   Engineered one the most daring prison breaks
   You found yourself in a gang
   Not just any gang, the ivory gang
   The notorious gang responsible for hundreds
   Of elephants and rhino's deaths
   Even the last fraction of principles
   Even that went out of the window
   You lived on the fringe of society
   This latest development
   Made yours a fully fledged criminal life
   And the news just couldn't stay away from the blackwidow
   Yet you were far from it
   You were just a lost soul
   Desperately trying to find a way out
   But for a fugitive on the run
   With a nationwide famous face like yours
   There was little point of redemption
   So you embraced it, the dark side of life
   It was easy money, most of the times
   Transportation was the biggest headache
   But you were a well oiled team
   And nothing happened in a long time
   Until a spectacular fallout
   Led the police straight to your hideout
   The blackwidow and her accomplices surrounded
   That was in the news for three days

Nobody was going down without a fight
So you all gave the police the fight they wanted
It rained bullets across the compound
Half the block was evacuated
And in the ensuing confusion a bullet
connected
It punctured through your abdomen
Caused massive internal bleeding
You had to surrender as the public watched
In dignified horror
Almost like an anticlimax to a movie
Yet again, the only survivor
But the future looked bleak, massive blood loss
Experts predicted this had to be the end
The final nail in the blackwidow's coffin

7. The sixth lease of life
Against all odds you survived
In recovery chained to a bed
Surrounded by a massive news crew
You were just happy to be alive
They thought you were defiant
You were laughing at the world
And their pathetic attempts to contain you
You were a criminal with a twist
Grossly exaggerated, dangerous from a
stranger's perspective
And still useful to the government
So they helped you disappear again
Right in front of the public's unbelieving eyes

A single gun from an unsuspecting officer
And a convincing tale from all those involved
And your profile truly reached legendary status
You were drafted to the U.S.A
For a special mission
To break down the global ivory trade
You had a resume to match
And still had contacts, it was easy to find your way
It was easy to fit in
Everyone had heard of the blackwidow
But that was just an imagination
The truth was a scared young woman
With absolutely no experience in deep cover
You played the game well
Cutting off contact with your handler
Waiting for the right moment
To bring down the house
But the more you waited, the harder it became
So you had a choice to make
And you made the only choice that made sense
You turned your back on the government
And were declared public enemy number one
You made a convincing act too, too convincing
That your own people were truly afraid
And the notorious gang leaders slept with one eye open.
They thought you could take it all
So they tried to eliminate the competition
In the most public way they could

A metro terminal crowded with commuters
A replay of the defiant message
And you in the toilet chained to a bomb vest
And then the explosion wrecked the terminal
A suicide bomber, the blackwidow
Had just caused the deaths of ninety seven
people
It was one for the history books
But that was it, history
The blackwidow was gone

8. The seventh lease of life
The blackwidow was not gone
But you liked it that way
You still found it odd that you were saved
A ten year old kid who idolized you
And was young enough to be swayed
On what was good and bad
It was not a conscious decision to let the place
blow
You were just out of time
The explosion was eminent
So you naturally chose self preservation
You were angry with how you were betrayed
Three days after the explosion, a kid shows up
At a police station with actual information
That leads to the arrest of seven unsuspecting
barons
The news started speculating
It had to be the blackwidow

And suddenly you had defied death, yet again
They contemplated you were taking over
The world of ivory trade yourself
They even listed you as the world's baddest woman
Such a profound honour
Then one day
Just when you were trying to put it all behind you
The police identified you in a ship
They thought you were smuggling in people
You were running away
So they stopped the ship, turned it upside down
They were looking for you
You had to choose between gunshot and drowning
You decided to go with drowning
The search helicopters hovered over the water
For hours waiting for you to surface
Nothing happened
This had to be the moment the blackwidow died
Ten minutes was too long even for you

9. The eighth lease of life
That was a narrow escape
Clever of you to use an officer to distract them
It was also cruel, cold and calculating
In a uniform of course no one

Not even the police themselves would have paid attention
Two weeks later the body is found
A female officer stabbed multiple times
The blackwidow survived yet again
And added one more officer to the list
You were back in the news in a major way
But you didn't even kill the officer, did you
In a ship like that, you couldn't be the only fugitive
The officer recognized someone
And paid with her life
What you found was a body that could be tossed
And a uniform that you could wear
So the largest manhunt was launched
It was time to put away the blackwidow
This time for good
That face, you had missed so much
Your little sister, all grown up
And there in the flesh
You couldn't believe your eyes
She was part of the task force
They thought a familiar face could lure you
She smiled at you then poisoned your drink
The first respondents confirmed you were dead
She was a hero to some, so selfless
And a villain to others, the fairytale was over
This time there was no mistaking
They did multiple tests to confirm it

The blackwidow was really dead

10. The ninth lease of life
You woke with coldness
Everything was cold, you were freezing
You were naked, confined, stiff, hungry and aching
The last thing you recalled
Was your sister smiling at you
And then your organs systematically shutting down
You should have been dead
So it was understandable why people freaked out
When a clotheless corpse wandered back into the news
Three days in a morgue
How could you be so resilient?
How could you not be dead?
The whole world watched you die
Have you been counting?
Your mind is not at a hundred
You are thinking about too much understanding little
There is a vehicle rushing towards you
I know you felt the impact
It was enough to make passers by cringe
It gave you impossible wings
You defied gravity, the collision echoed in the air
Long after the vehicle skidded to a stop

This could be just another brush with death
This could be the last of your nine lives
So what happens when the nine lives are over?

THE UNCONVENTIONAL MINDSET

1. A mind like yours thinks
   In black and white
   That life is a level field
   And the rate of success
   Is determined by the effort you make
   That the world cares for such things
   And there is good and evil
   And good will always triumph
   But a mind like yours
   Is young and naïve
   And is foolish to the reality of the world
   It is a jungle out there
   Only the fittest survive
   It is a man eat man world
   And there's no sense of justice at all

2. A mind like yours thinks
   That just like in the movies
   Life always turns out as planned
   That no matter how many times you fall
   You will always get one more chance
   To erase the past and set things right
   But a mind like yours
   Is young and naïve
   And is foolish to the reality of the world

Not everyone in life gets a second chance
In fact you have to be somebody to get a first chance

3. A mind like yours thinks
You can transcend who you are
You can defy the odds and rise above
You can be one in a million
You can be the one who makes it
Through hard work and dedication
You can get that manager's job
Or be the chief executive officer
You can have it all
But a mind like yours
Is young and naïve
And is foolish to the reality of the world
In a big company like that
There's always another one
Being groomed to replace
The one being groomed

4. A mind like yours thinks
If you have the courtesy to do good
Then people will do good to you
That no person has such a dark soul
That they would repay kind with vile
That when you read the Bible

And it says be good to your neighbours
Everyone reads the same Bible
So everyone knows to pay it forward
But a mind like yours
Is young and naïve
And is foolish to the reality of the world
People do what they want to do
Regardless of the rules or circumstances

5. A mind like yours thinks
If you find the one
Because you can find the one
The one who sweeps you off your feet
And you love each other
And they promise to be part of your life
Share forever with you
That you can be truly happy
But a mind like yours
Is young and naïve
And is foolish to the reality of the world
Love is not as strong as Hollywood paints it to be
People are strange, they always disappoint

6. A mind like yours thinks
That if you dream hard enough
If you keep that unwavering faith

You could be anything you want to be
A mind like yours thinks
If you keep writing
Keep on attending the writer's forums
Keep submitting drafts that matter
And you stay true to the course no matter
How many times they get thrown away
That you will be a great writer
That at some point in your career
You will be too good a writer
That the world will have no choice
But take notice
But a mind like yours
Is young and naïve
And is foolish to the reality of the world
The world can and most likely will ignore you
And keep on moving like you never mattered at
all

TO KILL A MOCKING BIRD

1. The mocking bird mocks
   With his flurry of feathers
   And his majestic poise
   Making such incoherent noise
   Though the master says he can talk
   He is a proud creature
   You can tell that by the way he struts
   Despite everything he is just a bird
   And where I come from whether it
   Chirps sings cries or howls
   If it looks like a bird it is a bird
   And birds are better food than company

2. The mocking bird mocks me
   See now that the master has left town
   He sits around all day
   Doing nothing, he doesn't leave his cage
   He never builds nests
   What a lazy bird he is
   He can't even find his own food
   Or clean his own cage
   I have to do it for him
   And it makes me sick to the pits of my
   stomach

3. The mocking bird mocks me

He makes a mess of the house
And make such noise when he is hungry
I am supposed to care that e is hungry
What kind of creature never grows up
My master says he should eat three times a
day
But since I don't have enough left
He has to do with one meal a day
If he doesn't like it, he can fly away
Like any other bird and get his own food

4. The mocking bird mocks me
Now he is even more lazy
He has even stopped strutting with pride
He lays on the same spot day after day
Even when I open the cage he doesn't go out
He expects me to feed him too
My life has become an empty meaning
That I have to feed a bird
The only kind of bird to be fed
Is a chicken that will one day be eaten

5. The mocking bird closed his eyes
Three days ago and refused to wake up
I know my master will come home one day
And he will be furious that his pet died
So I will pack this food he wastes

And be on my way out

Right from the moment I started, I couldn't stop I knew it was an obsession